the little book of BREATHWORK

First published in 2026 by OH
An Imprint of HEADLINE PUBLISHING GROUP LIMITED

1

Disclaimer:
This book is intended for general informational purposes only and should not be relied upon as recommending or promoting any specific practice, diet or method of treatment. It is not intended to diagnose, advise, treat or prevent any illness or condition and is not a substitute for advice from a professional practitioner of the subject matter contained in this book. You should not use the information in this book as a substitute for medication, nutritional, diet, spiritual or other treatment that is prescribed by your practitioner. Furthermore, the publisher is not affiliated with and does not sponsor or endorse any uses of or beliefs about in any way referred in this book.

Cataloguing in Publication Data is available from the British Library

ISBN 978-1-03543-354-4

Compiled and written by Lisa Pendreigh
Editorial: Beth Bishop and Victoria Denne
Designed and typeset in Joanna Sans Nova by Stephen Cary
Project manager: Russell Porter
Production Rachel Burgess
Printed and bound in Dubai

MIX
Paper | Supporting responsible forestry
FSC® C104740

Headline's policy is to use papers that are natural, renewable and recyclable products and made from wood grown in well-managed forests and other controlled sources. The logging and manufacturing processes are expected to conform to the environmental regulations of the country of origin.

HEADLINE PUBLISHING GROUP LIMITED
An Hachette UK Company
Carmelite House, 50 Victoria Embankment, London EC4Y 0DZ

The authorised representative in the EEA is Hachette Ireland, 8 Castlecourt Centre, Dublin 15, D15 XTP3, Ireland (email: info@hbgi.ie)

www.headline.co.uk www.hachette.co.uk

the little book of BREATHWORK

lisa pendreigh

CONTENTS

Introduction 6

Chapter 1

Debunking myths around breathwork 10

Chapter 2

Making a start 26

Chapter 3

Different types of breathwork 52

Chapter 4

Breathwork for the body 82

Chapter 5

Breathwork for the mind 110

Chapter 6

Breathwork for transformation 134

Chapter 7

Breathwork in daily life 162

INTRODUCTION

Breathing is an everyday miracle. Your body knows instinctively how to breathe, yet most people go through life without truly harnessing its power.

Breathwork draws on a wide spectrum of techniques – both ancient and modern – that intentionally guide the breath to calm the mind, energise the body or regulate emotions.

For centuries, cultures around the world have used breath-based techniques in martial arts, yoga, meditation and other healing traditions.

It offers a way to quieten external noise, return to your body and connect with what is already within you.

At its core, breathwork is about noticing how you breathe. Many of us take shallow, rapid breaths, especially when feeling anxious or rushed.

This can keep the body in a perpetual state of stress. By consciously slowing and deepening your breathing, you signal to your nervous system that you are safe, which helps the body relax.

Over time, this practice can calm the mind, increase energy levels and improve resilience.

If you are at the beginning of your breathwork journey, start slowly, listen to your body and approach the practices with openness and curiosity rather than impatience and expectation.

With consistency, breathwork can become a grounding tool to support everyday wellness and personal growth.

CHAPTER 1

DEBUNKING MYTHS around BREATHWORK

BREATHWORK is just DEEP BREATHING

This is not strictly true.

Some breathwork practices do require taking and holding deep breaths, but there are many more aspects and techniques involved.

Breathwork is far more intentional and varied – it's about consciously changing the **rhythm** and **pattern** of your breath to influence the body and mind.

BREATHWORK is a WOO-WOO WELLNESS TREND

Far from it! Controlled breathing techniques are thousands of years old. From yogic pranayama to Taoist qigong, breathing practices have been **key parts** of Eastern spiritual rituals for centuries.

However, breathwork has slowly become accepted as a healing practice in Western culture and outside of any religion or spirituality.

BREATHWORK is the SAME as MEDITATION

Breathwork and meditation do overlap in some respects.

However, breathwork is usually more active and about **physical** awareness, while meditation practice tends to be still and concentrates on **mental** focus.

Breathwork is often used as **preparation** for meditation by quieting the mind.

you have to SIT TOTALLY STILL during BREATHWORK

Breathwork can be woven into your everyday life, whether that is a moment of motionless calm or while carrying out daily chores.

There are many breathwork practices that involve **movement** – including yoga and qigong – and these are equally as valid.

BREATHWORK is PURELY SPIRITUAL

Spiritual practices, such as Buddhism, regard breath as the essence of life, and so incorporate breathing exercises.

At the same time, breathing is a **natural**, physiological function; modern science and medical research support the benefits of **controlled** breathing, making it a valid tool outside of spiritual realms.

BREATHWORK can be DANGEROUS

There are a number of breathing techniques that can be used without risk.

Everyday methods, such as Diaphragmatic Breathing or Box Breathing, are **safe** for beginners.

An advanced practice such as Holotropic Breathwork, which can bring on a trance-like state, must only be done with a trained facilitator.

BREATHWORK gives INSTANT RESULTS

Engaging in breathwork techniques can shift your physical or mental state within a short few minutes but, like meditation and exercise, it requires **consistent** practice to feel the long-term cumulative benefits.

Rather than being a one-off quick fix, breathwork should form part of a **regular** wellness routine.

BREATHWORK involves TAKING ON MORE OXYGEN

The goal of breathwork is not simply to up the percentage of oxygen in the body. In fact, over-breathing (or hyperventilation) can reduce the amount of oxygen delivered to the body's cells.

Controlled breathing is designed to **balance** the levels of oxygen and carbon dioxide, which is of greater benefit than just taking in "more air".

BREATHWORK is ONLY for DEALING WITH TRAUMA

Breathwork isn't only for people experiencing stress or trauma. It is beneficial for everyone.

Business professionals use it to improve focus. Athletes use it to **enhance** performance. Everyone can use it to cultivate calm in daily life.

BREATHWORK CAN HEAL ILLNESS

While breathwork can be used to **support** physical and emotional health by reducing stress and balancing the nervous system, it **does not** take the place of conventional medicine or professional counselling.

BREATHWORK is SOLELY for RELAXATION

While some breathing techniques **promote** calm, other techniques are designed to **energize**, release emotions or expand consciousness.

it is NORMAL to feel DIZZY DURING BREATHWORK

Sensations of dizziness can signal over-breathing (hyperventilation). Outside of a few specific guided breathwork methods, this is not necessarily desired.

If you feel lightheaded, **slow down** your breathing. Certain levels of discomfort (such as emotional release) can be part of the process, but experiencing pain or panic is a signal to stop.

remember:

- Breathwork is a simple yet powerful tool that bridges ancient wisdom and modern science, offering benefits for both body and mind.
- Breathwork is not a fad; rather it is a skilful practice that can bring great benefits.
- Like meditation or yoga, for many it is a lifelong practice that evolves with awareness.

"Breath is the power behind all things. I breathe in and know that good things will happen."

Tao Porchon-Lynch

Yoga master

CHAPTER 2

MAKING a START

WHAT do I NEED?

A safe, comfortable space

- Choose a quiet area free from distractions, where you feel safe and relaxed.
- Keep the space well ventilated with fresh air.
- Dim the lights or use natural lighting to create a calming atmosphere.
- Silence any devices: turn off your phone and mute any notifications.

A supportive mat, cushion or chair

- Comfort matters – your body should feel supported.
- When seated, use a yoga mat, meditation cushion or chair with good back support.
- When lying down, use a yoga mat, heavy blanket or padded floor space.

Cosy clothing and a light blanket

- Wear loose, non-restrictive clothing, made from natural, breathable fibres.
- Your body temperature can fluctuate during longer sessions, so have a light blanket to hand.

Soothing sounds and ambient atmosphere

- Gentle background music or guided audio can enhance relaxation and focus.
- Soundtracks with nature sounds or soft rhythms can help you stay present.
- Scented candles or essential oils can create a calming environment.

A drink of water

- Stay hydrated both before and after your breathwork session.
- Hydration supports your respiratory system, so keep a water bottle to hand.

Time and space to reflect

- Keep a journal or notebook hearby to note down any sensations or emotions that arise.
- After the session, you may want to turn your phone back on and use a breathwork app to track your practice.
- Journalling will help you track your progress over time.

An open mind

You don't need any expensive gear to practice breathwork. A quiet space, a comfortable position and a few mindful minutes are all you need to explore the power of your breath.

Approach breathwork with a non-judgemental attitude, maintain gentle curiosity and simply aim to be present rather than to strive for perfection.

how to START PRACTICING BREATHWORK

All breathwork begins with something simple yet profound: paying attention to your breath.

You have been breathing your entire life, but rarely with awareness. The moment you begin to consciously guide your breath, you start influencing your nervous system and your state of mind.

three REASONS to START PRACTICING BREATHWORK

1. reduce stress and anxiety

Breathwork enables you to consciously influence your nervous system, either activating it for energy and focus or calming it for peace and relaxation.

By adjusting the rhythm and depth of your breath, you can shift between the sympathetic nervous system (which increases the heart rate in preparation for stressful situations) and

the parasympathetic nervous system (which slows the heart rate and restores balance).

2. boost your mood naturally

Breathwork can release feel-good hormones including dopamine and serotonin. This natural chemical shift can uplift your mood.

3. release pent-up tension

Breathwork can release any stored tension or emotional residue. By accessing deeper layers of the nervous system, it helps to dissolve old stress patterns, leaving you feeling lighter and more centred.

OBSERVE your BREATH

Find a quiet place where you won't be disturbed. Wearing non-restrictive clothing, sit comfortably with your spine upright but relaxed.

Close your eyes and simply observe your natural breathing pattern.

Do not try to change it – simply notice how air feels as it enters your nostrils, fills your lungs and leaves your body. This gentle awareness is the foundation of all breathwork.

Most people are shallow breathers, using their upper chest instead of their diaphragm.

A dome-shaped muscle beneath the lungs, the diaphragm is the unsung hero of breathing as it does most of the work.

Shallow breathing underuses the diaphragm and reduces the amount of oxygen and carbon dioxide exchanged in a breath, which can contribute to stress and fatigue.

COHERENT breathing

Once you have observed your breath, experiment with slow, rhythmic breathing.

inhale through your nose
for a count of **5**

hold the breath
for a count of **2**

exhale gently through your nose
for a count of **5**

Practice for 5–10 minutes daily, ideally at the same time each day.

This simple technique helps balance the body's stress and relaxation responses.

As you progress, you can explore different styles of breathwork depending on your goals.

BOX breathing to calm anxiety

inhale through your nose

for a count of **4**

hold the breath

for a count of **4**

exhale gently through your nose

for a count of **4**

hold

for a count of **4**

Repeat these steps for 6 rounds.

4-7-8 breathing to promote relaxation

inhale through your nose
for a count of **4**

hold the breath
for a count of **7**

exhale gently through your nose
for a count of **8**

hold
for a count of **4**

Repeat these steps for 3 rounds.

alternate NOSTRIL breathing (Nadi Shodhana) to bring clarity to your mind

1. Use your right thumb to gently close your right nostril; inhale slowly through the left nostril
2. Close the left nostril with your ring finger, release the right nostril and exhale through the right
3. Inhale slowly through the right nostril
4. Close the right nostril, release the left nostril and exhale through the left

Repeat these steps for 5–10 minutes.

breath of FIRE (Kapalabhati)

to increase energy levels and clear mental fog

inhale gently through the nose

exhale quickly and forcefully through the nose by contracting your abdominal muscles and pumping your belly in and out

repeat this for 30 seconds – the inhales will occur naturally – then breathe normally for at least 60 seconds

Repeat these steps for up to 3 rounds.

Caution: This should be practiced on an empty stomach and avoided during pregnancy or for those with hypertension.

alternate EMBRYONIC breathing to restore vitality and find stillness

1. Sit with your hands resting on your lower abdomen
2. Allow your breath to become so gentle and subtle that it feels the body is breathing itself
3. Imagine you are breathing through your navel, as if connected to life by an umbilical cord
4. Stay with this mental image for as long as you like, relaxing deeply into each breath

FINISHING your practice

After practicing any breathwork technique, finish with an integration breath.

1. Take a few slow, deep belly breaths in through the nose and out through the mouth
2. While taking the breaths, place a hand on your heart and be aware of any feelings and emotions

be CONSISTENT

With any breathwork practice, start gently and build up gradually.

The key is consistency, not intensity. Even a few minutes a day can transform how you feel.

Approach breathwork with curiosity rather than control. Some days your breath will flow easily; on other days, it may feel shallow or uneven – both are part of the process.

Over time, you will discover that your breath is more than just a biological function – it is a

mirror.

Every **conscious breath** is an opportunity to **learn more** about yourself.

CHAPTER 3

DIFFERENT TYPES of BREATHWORK

The practice of breathwork is found across cultures and centuries, with each tradition using the breath to connect body, mind and spirit.

In the East, Taoist and qigong breathing cultivate *qi*, the vital life force that sustains health and harmony. Many indigenous and shamanic traditions use breath ceremonies to release emotion and connect with ancestral wisdom.

In Sufi mysticism, rhythmic breath and chanting create a path to divine union. In the Amazon, circular breathing rituals induce trances, while Native American chanting unites communities in healing and prayer.

Modern breathwork has evolved to meet the challenges of contemporary life – stress, overstimulation and disconnection. It has adapted into a goal-driven, accessible tool backed by medical research.

Through short, guided sessions, breathwork offers a healthy antidote to anxiety, trauma and isolation. By translating age-old practices into the language of modern life, breathwork bridges ancient wisdom and modern science.

YOGIC breathing (Pranayama)

origins: Pranayama is one of the oldest and most foundational forms of breathwork, originating from ancient India. The Sanskrit word *pranayama* combines *prana* (life force or vital energy) and *ayama* (expansion or control).

goal: To balance the body's energy, purify the mind and create harmony between the physical, mental and spiritual. It cultivates deeper states of awareness and stillness, while also calming the nervous system and supporting emotional regulation.

core techniques: Alternate Nostril Breathing for balance (page 46); Skull Shining Breath (Kapalabhati) for cleansing and energizing; Ocean Breath (Ujjayi) for focus and calm; and Humming Bee Breath (Bhramari) for soothing the mind.

intensity: Generally, gentle to moderate, depending on the technique. Can be energizing or relaxing, but always emphasizes awareness, control and balance, rather than force. Its power lies in its subtlety and consistency, not intensity.

TAOIST and QIGONG breathing

origins: Taoist and qigong breathing practices originate from ancient China, rooted in Taoist philosophy and traditional Chinese medicine. For thousands of years, these methods have been used to cultivate *qi* (the body's vital life energy).

goal: To nourish, circulate and balance *qi* throughout the body's energy channels (meridians) to promote vitality and emotional harmony. It emphasizes inner stillness and mind–body awareness rather than exertion or control.

core techniques: Diaphragmatic Breathing (page 100); Reverse Breathing (inhaling while drawing in the abdomen to strengthen internal energy); and Microcosmic Orbit Breathing (connecting the major energy centres through breath). The practice is often synchronized with slow, meditative movements and intention.

intensity: Generally gentle and meditative, Taoist and qigong breathing focuses on subtle energy flow rather than force. Its quiet depth makes it a sustainable, restorative practice that harmonizes body and spirit.

the WIM HOF method

origins: Developed by Dutch athlete Wim Hof, the method combines ancient yogic breathing practices with modern science. Hof discovered that through specific breath control, cold exposure and mindset training, humans could consciously influence their nervous system and stress response.

goal: To enhance physical resilience, mental focus and emotional balance. It helps reduce stress, strengthen immunity and increase energy. At a deeper level, it reconnects people with their innate ability to self-regulate.

core technique: Typically includes 30–40 deep, cyclic breaths, creating a wave-like rhythm. This is followed by a breath-retention phase, then a deep recovery breath, before repeating. The practice is often combined with cold-water immersion.

intensity: Moderate to intense, inducing strong physiological effects such as light-headedness, tingling and warmth. It is transformative, but should be practiced mindfully and never while driving.

HOLOTROPIC breathwork

origins: Holotropic Breathwork was developed in the 1970s by Dr Stanislav and Christina Grof – pioneering figures in transpersonal psychology. Drawing on ancient breathing traditions, modern psychology and music, their method uses the breath as a gateway to the unconscious.

goal: Emotional release, trauma healing and spiritual insight. By entering non-ordinary states, practitioners can access deep layers of memory, emotion and primal experience.

core techniques: Sessions are guided by facilitators and involve deep, continuous, accelerated breathing often accompanied by evocative music. Sessions may involve movement and emotional expression.

intensity: Intense and immersive. It can evoke strong physical, emotional and visionary experiences, resembling deep meditation or psychedelic journeys. It is powerful for trauma processing and self-discovery, but should be practiced only with a trained facilitator in a controlled environment.

REBIRTHING breathwork

origins: Rebirthing was developed in the 1970s by Leonard Orr, who believed that conscious breathing could release suppressed trauma. Rooted in Orr's own healing experiences, the practice evolved into a structured process blending spirituality, psychology and breath awareness.

goal: Emotional healing, self-acceptance and liberation from the subconscious. It helps dissolve limiting beliefs and unresolved memories stored in the body, promoting a sense of renewal, or "rebirth".

core techniques: Practitioners use connected circular breathing. This rhythmic flow increases oxygen, releases tension and allows repressed emotions to surface. Sessions often include guidance from a trained facilitator and time afterward to process insights.

intensity: Moderate to intense, depending on the individual. Experiences can range from gentle relaxation to powerful catharsis, making professional guidance essential. Guidance from a certified rebirthing facilitator is recommended.

TRANSFOR-MATIONAL breath

origins: Transformational breath combines conscious connected breathing with movement, sound and affirmations. Developed in the 1990s by Dr Judith Kravitz, the method involves continuous breathing while applying gentle pressure to open up restricted areas of the body.

Goal: Emotional integration, expanded consciousness and physical vitality. It helps release blocked energy, dissolve negative patterns and encourages connection.

The practice emphasizes using the breath as a tool for self-healing.

core techniques: Connected circular breathing through the mouth, supported by affirmations, gentle movement and toning (vocal sound) to amplify energy flow. Facilitators may apply light touch to areas of physical tension to help open the breath pattern and release emotional blockages.

intensity: Ranges from moderate to high intensity. Sessions can be cathartic and deeply healing. It's often practiced in workshops or private sessions and can lead to profound emotional breakthroughs.

SHAMANIC breathing (or conscious connected breathing)

origins: With roots in ancient indigenous and tribal traditions from around the world, including Amazonian, Andean and Native North American practices, rhythmic breath, drumming and chanting are used to enter trance states and connect with spirits.

This approach has merged with contemporary methods such as Rebirthing and Holotropic Breathwork.

goal: To access expanded states of awareness, release emotional blockages and reconnect with intuition and the sacred. It supports physical, emotional and spiritual healing.

core techniques: Often practiced in group ceremonies, this approach uses continuous circular breathing often alongside drumming or guided intention. Rhythm and sound help sustain an altered yet conscious state.

intensity: Typically intense and immersive, evoking vivid sensations, emotions and spiritual experiences. Best practiced in a facilitated setting, it should be approached with respect due to its intensity.

BUDDHIST MINDFULNESS

origins: *Anapanasati*, or "mindfulness of breathing", originates from the teachings of the Buddha, over 2,500 years ago. It serves as a foundation for mindfulness practices found across many Buddhist traditions.

goal: To develop mindfulness, calm the mind and cultivate insight (*vipassana*) into the nature of reality. By observing the breath, one learns to witness thoughts and sensations without attachment, fostering emotional balance and mental clarity.

core techniques: Centres on simply observing the natural breath – its rhythm, texture and the subtle sensations of inhalation and exhalation. Attention is often placed on the nostrils or the rise and fall of the abdomen.

intensity: Gentle and contemplative, making it ideal for daily use. Nonetheless, it is profound in its potential to transform awareness and bring inner peace.

BUTEYKO breathing

origins: Developed in the 1950s by Ukrainian physician Dr Konstantin Buteyko, who created a method to retrain breathing patterns and restore optimal respiratory function. First used to treat asthma, it was later applied to anxiety, sleep disorders and stress-related conditions.

goal: To normalize breathing volume, enhance oxygen delivery and calm the nervous system. Slower, lighter nasal breathing maintains proper carbon dioxide levels, supporting better energy, concentration and emotional stability.

core techniques: Nasal breathing, reduced breathing exercises and breath-hold control tests. The emphasis is on gentle, quiet and minimal breathing, rather than deep or forceful inhalations.

intensity: Gentle and therapeutic; subtle yet powerful. It emphasizes mindfulness and consistency over exertion. Regular practice can cultivate calm and resilience, making it ideal for modern stress management.

COHERENT breathing

origins: A modern, science-based breathwork method developed in the early 2000s by Stephen Elliott and later supported by research from Dr Richard Brown and Dr Patricia Gerbarg. It draws from yoga, neuroscience and physiology.

goal: To create harmony between the heart, lungs and nervous system. By synchronizing breath rhythm with the body's natural oscillations, it helps to reduce anxiety, improve focus, lower blood pressure and enhance overall wellbeing.

core techniques: Breathing at a slow, even pace – typically 5–6 breaths per minute (see page 42). Breathing is gentle, nasal and diaphragmatic, with no holding or force.

intensity: Gentle and deeply calming; suitable for all levels. Its simplicity makes it easy to integrate into daily routines, offering a grounding antidote to modern stress and overstimulation.

BOX breathing

origins: Also known as Square Breathing, this method has roots in ancient yogic techniques but gained modern prominence through its use by Navy SEALs as a tool for composure under pressure.

goal: To calm the nervous system and enhance emotional control. The even rhythm created between breaths and retention balances oxygen and carbon dioxide levels, helping shift your system from stress (sympathetic) to relaxation (parasympathetic). It is highly effective for managing anxiety and panic.

core techniques: Breathing is slow, nasal and diaphragmatic (see page 44 for directions). The "box" represents the steady, balanced nature of the rhythm.

intensity: Gentle yet focused; accessible for beginners and powerful for professionals in high-stress environments. When practiced for just a few minutes, it will quickly induce calm and clarity.

Before moving forward,
remember that:

every
breath

is a chance to
shift your **body**,
mind
and **emotions**.

Breathing is **not** passive.
It is a
powerful
active tool
that is
waiting to be **used**
with
awareness.

remember:

• Breathwork spans a wide range of techniques – from gentle, regulating practices, to transformative, high-intensity methods.

• Each style meets different needs. Together, they reveal the breath's universal power – a tool for both stability and transformation, guiding us toward greater presence, connection and self-understanding.

"Breath is the link between the mind and body."

B.K.S. Iyengar

Yoga guru

CHAPTER 4

BREATHWORK for the BODY

Your body is a living system of myriad functions – and at the centre of it all is breathing. You can go weeks without food, days without water, but only minutes without air. This simple fact highlights how breath is the foundation of health.

Whether called *prana* in India, *qi* in China, *ruach* in Hebrew or *pneuma* in Greek, breath has long been described as the vital life force.

Most people breathe poorly. Sedentary lifestyles, slouched posture and shallow breathing rob the body of its natural efficiency.

Breathwork can energize the body, restore balance and enhance performance.

Whether your goal is to improve your posture, increase your physical endurance or simply to feel better in yourself, the way you breathe matters.

Breathing is not just about getting oxygen in; it is also about balancing the *levels* of oxygen and carbon dioxide in the body.

Oxygen fuels cellular energy production, while carbon dioxide regulates blood pH and signals to your body when it needs to breathe.

A common misconception is that carbon dioxide is simply the waste product of breathing. In reality, the right level of carbon dioxide is essential to the process.

When you exhale too quickly or too forcefully (hyperventilation), your carbon dioxide level drops, leading to dizziness, tingling and even panic.

On the other hand, controlled breathing increases carbon dioxide slightly, which can dilate blood vessels, improve circulation and enhance oxygen delivery to tissues.

"Good posture can be successfully acquired only when the entire mechanism of the body is under perfect control. Graceful carriage follows as a matter of course from proper breathing."

Joseph Pilates

Physical trainer

BREATH, POSTURE and ALIGNMENT

Posture and breath are codependent.

Poor posture means a slouched back, hunched shoulders and collapsed chest, which restrict lung expansion and increase tension and fatigue.

Correct breathing expands the ribs, drops the shoulders, lifts the chest and strengthens the diaphragm, naturally encouraging an upright posture.

seated ALIGNMENT breath

A simple yet effective exercise that improves both breath and posture. It retrains the diaphragm, strengthens the core, promotes upright posture and connects breath to spinal support – the foundation of healthy movement, calm focus and confident presence.

It is suitable and safe for anyone to try. With each cycle, imagine your breath creating more space and stability in your body.

1. Sit tall. Imagine a string gently lifting the crown of your head toward the ceiling. Let your shoulders drop and your chest open.
2. Align and relax. Tuck in your chin to lengthen the back of your neck. Feel your spine lengthening, balanced over your hips.
3. Inhale slowly through your nose. Let the air expand your lower ribs and belly (not your chest). Feel your spine elongate and your chest open.
4. Exhale gently through your nose. Feel your shoulder blades drop and your body ground itself into the chair or cushion.

Repeat these steps for 5–10 breaths.

BREATH and PHYSICAL PERFORMANCE

Athletes rely on breath control as part of their training and performance.

According to modern sports science, breath directly influences stamina, power and recovery.

Breathing can delay the buildup of lactic acid in the muscles, increase carbon dioxide tolerance and improve oxygen utilization, all of which significantly improve endurance.

Elite sportsmen and women integrate breathwork into their training routines and regard it to be just as crucial as physical conditioning.

BREATH, ENERGY and STAMINA

Many people feel tired not through a lack of sleep but because of inefficient breathing.

Rapid, shallow breathing can leave you under-oxygenated; while slow, steady breathing boosts cellular energy production.

This is why breathwork is often described as "charging the body".

"Controlled deep breathing helps the body to transform the air we breathe into energy."

Nancy Zi

Singer and breathwork teacher

ENERGIZING breath

This simple, science-backed breathing exercise boosts energy and stamina.

It stimulates circulation, oxygenates the brain and activates the sympathetic nervous system, giving you a natural energy boost. It also trains your diaphragm for better breathing and improved stamina over time.

It's easy to do whenever you need an energy injection.

sit or stand tall. Keep your spine upright and your shoulders relaxed. Engage your core.

inhale actively. Breathe in through your nose quickly and fully, feeling your ribs and belly expand.

exhale gently, out through your nose without pushing or using force.

find a rhythm. Try one inhale and one exhale per second.

Take 10–20 breaths, then pause and breathe normally for 30 seconds.

Repeat these steps for 2–3 rounds.

BREATH and STRESS in the BODY

Physical health is not just about conditioning the organs and muscles; it is also about how your body responds to stress.

Chronic stress keeps the body in a state of hyper-alertness: an elevated heart rate, tight muscles and shallow breathing.

Over time, this contributes to high blood pressure, inflammation and weakened immunity.

Slow, deep breathing counteracts hyper-alertness.

By stimulating the vagus nerve (the body's main parasympathetic pathway), breathwork lowers the heart rate, dilates the blood vessels and reduces cortisol levels.

What starts as a simple exhale can ripple through every system of the body, improving long-term health.

DIAPHRAGMATIC
breathing

This is the cornerstone of all breathwork. It strengthens the diaphragm, improves lung capacity and reduces tension in the body.

1. Lie on your back with your knees bent and feet on the floor
2. Place one hand on your chest, the other on your belly
3. Inhale so the belly hand rises while the chest hand stays relatively still
4. Exhale slowly

Repeat these steps for 5–10 minutes.

NASAL breathing

Breathing through the nose (rather than the mouth) filters, warms and humidifies air.

It also produces nitric oxide, a molecule that dilates blood vessels and improves oxygen delivery.

Try spending a day breathing only through your nose – even during exercise – and notice the difference in your energy levels and clarity of thinking.

COHERENT breathing

Breathing at a rhythm of about 6 breaths per minute synchronizes heart-rate variability and promotes whole-body balance.

This technique of inhaling for 5 seconds, then exhaling for 5 seconds is especially effective for lowering blood pressure and calming the nervous system.

(See also page 42).

the WIM HOF method

At its core, the Wim Hof Method shows how breath can push the body beyond perceived limits, unlocking hidden reserves of strength.

It has inspired millions to rethink what is possible through conscious breathing.

(See also page 60).

SLEEP breathing

Breathing can be the gateway to deeper sleep. The 4–7–8 Breathing method (see page 45) activates the parasympathetic system, lowering the heart rate and quieting the mind.

Practiced regularly, it helps reduce anxiety and insomnia as it slows the heart rate and prepares the body for rest.

Consistency brings cumulative calm, training your body to shift naturally into a state of ease.

PAIN in the BODY

The techniques of Diaphragmatic Breathing (see page 100) and Coherent Breathing (see page 42) can lessen chronic pain in the body as the muscles relax through proper breath support.

Breathwork may not cure a physical condition, but it is a useful tool to manage pain and reduce suffering.

breath as PREVENTIVE MEDICINE

Breathwork can lower stress, reduce blood pressure, improve digestion, enhance sleep and boost immunity, all without side effects.

While it's not a replacement for conventional medical treatment, it is a powerful preventive tool. It equips the body to handle stress, improves circulation and creates the physiological conditions for healing.

DAILY breath RESET

This 15-minute reset can dramatically improve your energy levels, your overall mood and your sleep quality.

morning: 5 minutes of **box** breathing, for energy (see page 44)

afternoon: 5 minutes of **coherent** breathing, for balance (see page 42)

evening: 5 minutes of **4–7–8** breathing, for rest (see page 45)

remember:

• Breath is the foundation of physical wellbeing.

• It shapes posture, fuels performance, regulates stress and supports recovery.

• Most importantly, it can always be accessed. Unlike medicine or equipment, you carry this tool with you everywhere.

"The breath is the bridge which connects life to consciousness, which unites your body to your thoughts."

Thich Nhat Hanh

Buddhist monk

CHAPTER 5

BREATHWORK for the MIND

As you deepen your practice, you may notice that breath not only strengthens the body, but also clears the mind. Breathwork is a tool not just for physical health, but also for mental clarity and emotional balance.

When thoughts race, emotions surge and stress rises, the breath responds accordingly: quick, shallow breaths accompany anxiety, while slow, deep breaths reflect calm.

And the connection works both ways – by changing your breath, you can change your mindset.

Breathing is unique in that it is both automatic and voluntary. You can forget all about it and still your body will keep you alive. But you can also consciously change your breathing pattern – not something you can do with, say, your heartbeat or digestion.

The breath is like a remote control for the nervous system. It gives you a direct, accessible way to influence your mental and emotional state by retuning to another channel.

By learning to harness this connection, you can reduce anxiety, sharpen focus, enhance creativity and cultivate emotional resilience.

breath and MODERN-DAY STRESS

Life is saturated with stressors – work deadlines, social pressures, financial worries to name a few – but the body's nervous system evolved for survival in a different world, one when "fight or flight" responses were triggered by wild animals, not unread emails.

Nowadays, many of us are stuck in a low-grade stress state, breathing shallowly and rapidly without even realizing it. This stimulates the sympathetic nervous system, keeping the mind agitated.

Breathwork is a way to reclaim control. By shifting your breathing pattern, you can literally flip a switch in your brain, moving from anxiety towards calm and from distraction towards clarity.

Although it makes up only 2 per cent of your body weight, the brain consumes about 20 per cent of your body's oxygen supply.

Small changes in breathing can significantly impact cognition and mood.

breath and FOCUS

Breath has a profound effect on your ability to maintain attention. Ancient meditation traditions recognized this and modern neuroscience confirms it.

Slow, rhythmic breathing synchronizes brainstem, limbic system (emotion) and prefrontal cortex (thinking) activity, which enhances focus and decision-making.

Alternate Nostril Breathing (page 46) can balance activity between areas of the brain, improving cognitive performance, while breath-holding exercises increase tolerance to discomfort, training the mind to stay steady under pressure.

focus your

breath

and your breath will

focus your

mind.

breathwork and EMOTIONS

Your breath does not just *reflect* your emotional state – it shapes it. Stress triggers short, quick breaths; while consciously slowing your breathing helps reduce stress.

The loop can go either way: spiralling into tension or expanding into calm. Recognizing this connection is the first step toward mastering breathwork. Emotions and breathing are inseparable.

By noticing and guiding your breath, you can learn to navigate emotions skilfully rather than be engulfed by them.

the long EXHALE

When you exhale for longer than you inhale, you activate the parasympathetic nervous system, the body's natural "rest and digest" response. This simple shift can turn rising anxiety into a sense of calm within minutes.

try it:

inhale

for a count of 4

exhale

for a count of 6 or 8.

Notice how your mood shifts as the breath slows the mind.

breathwork for MENTAL HEALTH

Breathing methods are often used to help anxiety disorders, depression, post-traumatic stress disorder and trauma, through:

physiological regulation: controlled breath lowers the heart rate and blood pressure, reducing physical symptoms of anxiety.

emotional release: certain breath practices can bring suppressed emotions to the surface, allowing safe processing.

mind-body awareness: tuning into the breath helps reconnect with the body, grounding in the present moment.

"Feelings come and go like clouds in a windy sky. Conscious breathing is my anchor."

Thich Nhat Hanh

Buddhist monk

COHERENT breathing for CALM

This practice reduces mental chatter and restores balance. It helps calm the body through its effect on the autonomic nervous system, making it especially useful before stressful meetings or at the end of a long, frantic day.

Technique reminder (see page 42):

inhale for a count of 5

hold the breath for a count of 2

exhale for a count of 5

Repeat these steps for 10–15 minutes.

extended EXHALE for ANXIETY

This technique activates the vagus nerve and quiets anxiety.

inhale gently through the nose for a count of 4

exhale slowly through pursed lips for a count of 8

Repeat these steps for 5 minutes.

breath of CLARITY (bellows breath)

Use this technique when you feel sluggish or mentally foggy. Adapted from yoga's *bhastrika*, this energizing practice wakes up the mind.

sit tall

inhale forcefully through the nose

exhale forcefully through the nose

Repeat these steps at a steady pace for 20–30 breaths.

BOX breathing for FOCUS

This technique redirects your attention away from distractions and trains the mind to concentrate. With regular practice, box breathing can enhance your ability to stay focused on everyday tasks.

Technique reminder (see page 44):

inhale for a count of 4

hold for a count of 4

exhale for a count of 4

hold for a count of 4

Repeat these steps for 3–5 minutes.

mindfully OBSERVE your BREATH

The simplest yet most profound breathwork practice is just to notice. This builds awareness and teaches the mind to rest in the present moment.

Consciously observe the inhale and exhale of your breath without trying to change it.

"The pattern of your breathing affects the pattern of your performance. When you are under stress, deep breathing helps bring your mind and body back into the present."

Gary Mack

Voice actor

breathwork and CREATIVITY

Breathing doesn't just calm the mind; it can expand it.

Altering breathing patterns changes brainwave activity, sometimes shifting from beta (normal waking mode) into alpha or even theta states, which are associated with creativity and insight.

Writers, artists and musicians have long used rhythmic breathing before any creative endeavours.

CREATIVE breath

sit tall with your eyes closed

inhale slowly through the nose, imagining inspiration entering your body with the breath

exhale slowly, visualizing any creative blocks and doubts exiting with the breath

Repeat these steps for 5 minutes, then begin your creative work.

breathwork and RESILIENCE

Life is unpredictable. Stressful events are unavoidable. But resilience – the ability to recover and adapt – can be strengthened through breath.

By practicing breathwork under controlled conditions (such as breath-holding or fast breathing), you teach the mind to stay calm in discomfort.

Over time, this resilience extends to real-life challenges.

breath for the MIND

This short 10-minute routine can be used to stabilize your mental state and reset your entire day.

1 Consciously observe your **natural breathing** for 2 minutes without trying to affect it

2 Practice **box breathing** for 3 minutes (see page 44)

3 Practice an **extended exhale** for 3 minutes (see page 119)

4 Practice 2 minutes of **stillness**, simply noticing how your mind feels

remember:

Your breath is the key to mastering your inner landscape. With it, you can calm anxiety, sharpen focus, release emotions and even spark creativity.

As you bring breathwork into your daily life, your relationship with thoughts and feelings may begin to shift. Rather than being consumed by every wave of emotion, you start to steer the current through your breath.

"Breathing is a lot like creativity. Like an inhale, you receive an inspiration, you let it run through the unique magnificence of who you are, and then you release it into the world, letting it go, unattached to the way it needs to look."

Jill Badonsky

Artist

CHAPTER 6

BREATHWORK for TRANS-FORMATION

the TRANSFORMATIVE POWER of breath

Breath can support physical and mental health, but it can also act as a catalyst for healing and profound inner transformation and growth.

Beyond sustaining the body or steadying the mind, breath has the power to shift you at your core.

Around the world, people have discovered that specific breathing practices can release trauma, ease emotional wounds, awaken inner strength and even open doorways to profound spiritual or cosmic experiences.

Modern medicine increasingly acknowledges what ancient traditions have long understood: breath is not just physiological.

It is a tool for accessing deeper layers of the psyche and the body's innate capacity to heal.

breath and TRAUMA

Trauma lives not only in memory, but also in the body. Muscles tense, breathing becomes shallow and the nervous system stays on high alert.

For some, this pattern can last for years. Breathwork offers a gentle way to release this stored tension.

By working with the breath, the body can begin to unlock suppressed emotions and allow them to surface and be processed safely.

Research on trauma recovery shows that techniques such as deep, rhythmic breathing can shift the nervous system out of survival mode and into a state of healing.

Many people who practise breathwork report tears, laughter, trembling or waves of release – as the body lets go of what it has held.

HOLOTROPIC
breathwork

One of the most influential modern systems for transformation is Holotropic Breathwork (see also page 62), which was designed as an alternative to psychedelic therapy after research using the hallucinogenic LSD was restricted.

Conducted in a safe, supervised environment, deep, rapid breathing is practiced over an extended period, accompanied by evocative music.

This practice often induces non-ordinary states of consciousness where participants may revisit memories or experience symbolic visions. While intense, the process can lead to profound emotional release.

Holotropic Breathwork bypasses the analytical mind and allows unconscious material to surface.

The breath becomes a bridge between body, psyche and spirit, facilitating integration and healing.

REBIRTHING
breathwork

Rebirthing Breathwork uses continuous, circular breathing, with no pauses between inhale and exhale (see also page 64).

This pattern is designed to help access the subconscious, where memories, emotions and physical sensations can more easily surface.

Many people report revisiting and resolving birth trauma and other early-life imprints through this type of breathwork.

While controversial at times, rebirthing underscores the idea that early experiences – and the breath patterns formed around them – shape us deeply.

By consciously re-patterning the breath, individuals can reshape their inner lives.

the WIM HOF method (Simplified)

This technique boosts energy and resilience but should always be practiced in a safe environment.

1. Take **30 deep breaths** in and out, inhaling fully and exhaling without force
2. After the last exhale, **hold your breath** as long as comfortable
3. **Inhale fully**, hold for 15 seconds, then release

Repeat these steps for 3–4 rounds.

"Breathing exercises produce brain waves."

Wim Hof

Extreme athlete

SHAMANIC
breathing practices

Beyond Asia, indigenous cultures around the world have long used breath in rituals of healing, initiation and connection with the spirit world.

Shamans use rhythmic breathing, often paired with drumming or chanting, to enter altered states of consciousness where they seek guidance, healing or correspondence with ancestors.

In these traditions, breath is the pulse that connects individuals to their community, lineage and the natural world.

For participants, such breath ceremonies can be profoundly transformative – releasing grief, restoring a sense of belonging or inducing visions that reframe life's challenges.

These practices remind us that healing unfolds not only within the individual, but within the collective too.

breath and SPIRITUAL AWAKENING

Beyond strengthening the body or healing trauma, breath has long been used as a doorway to spiritual awakening.

Yogic pranayama, Taoist inner alchemy, Tibetan tummo and Christian contemplative prayer all recognize breath as a vehicle for transcending ordinary consciousness.

Spiritual breath practices often share common themes:

- **Expansion** – breath becomes a focus that leads beyond the self.
- **Purification** – old patterns of thinking are released through controlled breathing.
- **Union** – breath is experienced as the flow of universal life force, connecting the individual to the cosmos.

For some, these practices evoke mystical experiences – a sense of unity or deep peace. For others, the transformation is more grounded, showing up as greater presence and ease in daily life.

CIRCULAR

connected breathing

This method can bring buried emotions and memories to the surface. Allow them to rise without judgement, trusting your breath to carry you through.

lie down comfortably

inhale fully through the nose

exhale immediately through the mouth and begin the next inhale without pause

Repeat these steps at a steady rhythm for 10–20 minutes.

TRANS-FORMATIONAL

breath pattern

This pattern expands lung capacity and opens emotional channels.

inhale deeply into the belly, chest and upper chest in one wave

exhale with a sigh, releasing tension

Continue for 10 minutes, gradually deepening the breath.

SAFETY and PREPERATION

Transformational breath practices are powerful and should be approached with respect. Because they can evoke intense emotions or physical sensations, it's important to:

Practice in a **safe**, supportive environment

Work with a **trained** facilitator for deeper sessions

Avoid advanced techniques if you have certain medical conditions (cardiovascular issues, epilepsy, pregnancy), unless guided by a professional

the UNIVERSAL experience

Despite cultural differences, many traditions share common threads in their use of breathwork, including:

- Breath as **life force** – not merely a process of oxygen exchange.
- Breath as a **bridge**, connecting body and mind, physical and spiritual.
- Breath for **transformation**, capable of purifying and healing.
- Breath as **ritual**, linking the individual to the community and cosmos.

The universality of
these insights suggests
that humanity
understands that breath
is a doorway
to dimensions of
experience beyond
the ordinary.

breathwork
can
open
doors,
but must be
practiced
responsibly

the INTEGRATION process

Breathwork sessions often bring insights, emotions or visions, but the true transformation happens in *integration* – how you apply those experiences to your life.

Journalling, using an app, sharing with a trusted friend or simply sitting in stillness can help anchor the lessons.

Healing is not just about release; it's about weaving new ways of being. Breath may spark the shift, but your daily choices sustain it.

remember:

Breath is more
than survival – it is medicine
for the soul.

Through practices
old and new you can heal
wounds, release what
no longer serves you
and step into a fuller version
of yourself.

Transformation through breath is not about escaping reality, but about returning to it with renewed strength and clarity.

As you continue your journey, remember that the breath is always with you: an ally, a healer and a guide.

"Breath is a powerful tool that we have to help us manage stress, calm our thoughts, and transform our experience."

Dr Andrew Weil

Doctor

"The pause between breathing in and breathing out is the doorway to mystery."

Ojibway elder

CHAPTER 7

BREATHWORK in DAILY LIFE

a WAY of LIFE

As we saw in the last chapter, real transformation doesn't come from a single session or a workshop, but through integration.

So, how can breathwork become not just a practice, but a way of living?

integration is about weaving breathwork into the fabric of daily life – so it's not an activity you do, but a way you *are*.

This chapter offers strategies, practices and routines to make breathwork sustainable, accessible and deeply personal.

in the MORNING: breathwork as a RESET BUTTON

How you breathe when you wake sets the tone for your day.

Instead of rushing into tasks or grabbing your phone, start with a few minutes of conscious breathing.

Morning ritual

(5–10 minutes)

This simple routine will boost your energy, regulate your nervous system and give you a calm, intentional start.

1. Sit upright in bed or on the floor
2. Take 10 deep, diaphragmatic breaths, waking up the body (see page 100)
3. Practice 2–3 minutes of Coherent Breathing (see page 42)
4. With one final deep inhale and exhale, set your intention for the day

at WORK: breathwork as a PRODUCTIVITY TOOL

Modern workplaces are filled with stress triggers. Left unchecked, shallow breathing can dominate the day, reduce focus and increase fatigue.

Integrating short breathwork practices into your work hours can shift everything.

Quick resets

(5–10 minutes)

1. Between meetings or before a presentation, take 2 minutes to breathe at 5–6 breaths per minute. This steadies your heart rate, calms nerves and sharpens focus.

2. Turn routine walks – bathroom breaks, lunchtimes – into micro-breathwork practices.

3. Try syncing your breath with your steps – for example, inhale for 4 steps, exhale for 6 steps. This can ground you throughout the day.

at HOME: breathwork for CONNECTION

Breathwork is not only personal, it is relational. Breathing together strengthens connection with loved ones.

family breathing:

Take a few minutes to sit together and breathe slowly. Children especially benefit from learning to calm themselves this way.

partner practice:

Sit facing each other, breathing in sync. This fosters intimacy and presence.

conflict reset:

When tension rises, pause for a few deep breaths before responding.

EVENING: breathwork for REST and RECOVERY

The body restores itself during sleep, but many people take the stress of the day to bed with them.

Breathwork can open the door to restorative rest.

Wind-down

(10 minutes)

This simple ritual signals safety to your nervous system and prepares you for deeper sleep.

1 Sit or lie comfortably

2 Practice 4–7–8 Breathing (see page 45) for 5 rounds

3 Transition into gentle Diaphragmatic Breathing (see page 100), letting the exhale lengthen naturally

2 End with gratitude: inhale with the thought "thank you", then exhale with release

breath and MOVEMENT

Integration doesn't mean always sitting still and reflecting on your breathwork practice. In fact, breathwork pairs beautifully with movement.

Breath becomes the invisible partner in every movement, enhancing performance and awareness.

- **Yoga:** link each movement to an inhale or exhale, as in sun salutations.
- **Walking or running:** experiment with nasal breathing to improve endurance.
- **Strength training:** exhale during exertion, inhale during release. Proper breathing stabilizes the core and prevents injury.
- **Dance or martial arts:** notice how breath powers rhythm, grace and timing.

creating a PERSONAL PRACTICE

Your breathwork practice needs to fit around you – your schedule, needs and goals. When you breathe with intention amid your day's rhythm, a single moment can become a sanctuary.

Here are five steps to help you design a practice that you can easily incorporate into your daily routine.

1 Start small: even 5 minutes daily creates change. Think consistency over duration.

2 Choose a few core techniques: try Coherent Breathing (see page 42) for balance, Box Breathing (see page 44) for focus and Extended Exhale (see page 119) for relaxation.

2 Anchor to existing habits/routines, such as after brushing your teeth, before opening your laptop and as you are heading to bed.

4 Track progress: journal how you feel. Over time, patterns will show the benefits.

5 Stay flexible: some days may call for energizing breath, others for calming. Adapt to what your body and mind need.

breathwork for EVERYDAY CHALLENGES

Breathwork offers a reliable, always-available toolkit for navigating both the expected and the unexpected.

Practiced regularly, these techniques become instinctive, ready to support you whenever you need them most.

- For **morning fatigue:** practice Bellows Breath (see page 124) or 30 deep inhalations to boost energy.
- For **interrupted sleep:** practice 4–7–8 Breathing (see page 45) to quiet the mind.
- During an **anxiety spike:** use Extended Exhale Breathing (see page 119) to reset the nervous system.
- Before **public speaking:** practice 3 minutes of Box Breathing (see page 44) for calm focus.
- When **stuck in traffic:** reduce frustration with Coherent Breathing (see page 42).

breathwork as a LIFELONG JOURNEY

Integrating breathwork into everyday life is not about achieving perfection. It's about cultivating a relationship with your breath that grows and evolves.

Some days your practice may feel deep and transformative; other days, it may feel ordinary or unremarkable. Both are valuable.

Over time, breathwork can shift from being something you have to schedule into your day to being something you live. You will notice it in how you walk into a room, how you handle stress, how you connect with others, how you rest at night.

Journalling prompts for reflection and integration

Journalling after breathwork can deepen insight, integrate emotions and help track subtle shifts in body and mind.

body awareness prompts

1. What physical sensations did I notice during my breathwork practice?
2. Where in my body did I feel tension?
3. How did my energy change before, during and after the session?
4. What did my body seem to be telling me?

emotional exploration prompts

5 What emotions surfaced during my practice?

6 Did any memories, images or feelings unexpectedly arise?

7 How did I respond to any discomfort or intensity?

6 What emotion feels most present in me right now?

mindful insight prompts

9 What thoughts or realizations came through in the stillness?

10 Did my mind resist, relax or wander?

11 What patterns in my thinking or breathing did I notice?

12 What lesson or truth feels clearer after this session?

integration and intention prompts

13 How do I feel now, physically, emotionally and mentally?

14 What do I want to carry forward from this experience?

15 What small action or shift will help me build on what I felt today?

16 How might my breath guide me through the rest of my day or week?

Reflection transforms seemingly scattered breathwork practices into a conscious journey.

breath as a DAILY COMPANION

At its core, integration means recognizing that your breath is always with you. Wherever you are, you can return to the breath. It is the most portable, reliable and personal tool you will ever have. Instead of overhauling your schedule, it is possible to integrate short breathwork breaks into even the busiest life.

You don't need "additional" time, but to simply shift your breathing during existing moments in your day.

the invitation is simple:
let breath be your
constant
companion
reminding you to
slow down, to focus,
to connect, to
release.

remember:

Breathwork is not about escape;
it is about presence.

It brings you into your body,
into the moment and into life itself.

When integrated into daily living,
breathwork becomes a quiet
revolution – shaping how you handle
stress, connect with others and
move through the world.

"Your breath is your ancient friend."

Thich Nhat Hanh

Buddhist monk

This is not the end of your journey, but the beginning of a lifelong relationship with the breath.

Every inhale and exhale is an opportunity to reset, to heal, to transform.

And every breath is a reminder: you are alive, here and now.

"Breathing is the first act of life, and the last. Our very life depends on it."

Joseph Pilates

Physical trainer

Breath is at once ordinary and everyday, but also abstract and mystical.

Breath is **life.**

It is through your reconnection to your own breath that you can define and experience for yourself what your **breathwork** is.